PENGUIN WORKSHOP
An imprint of Penguin Random House LLC, New York

First published in the United States of America by Penguin Workshop,
an imprint of Penguin Random House LLC, New York, 2023

Visit us online at penguinrandomhouse.com.

Library of Congress Cataloging-in-Publication Data is available.

Manufactured in China

ISBN 9780593522332   10 9 8 7 6 5 4 3 2 1 TOPL

Design by DGPH Studio

Amazing
INSECTS
Around the World

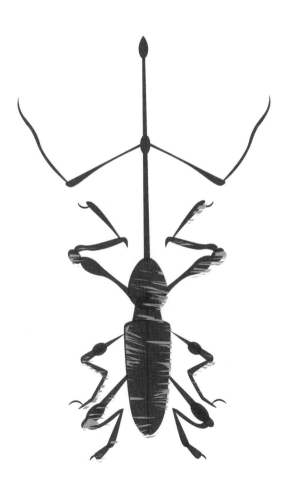

by DGPH Studio

Contents

Our Planet

Insects are, without a doubt, one of the most wonderful and varied life-forms on our planet. Since life appeared on earth, insects and bugs have existed, spreading plant seeds, digging tunnels to bring air to the soil and create channels for water, helping to break down dead animals, and providing a source of food for other animals.

They can be as tiny as a pinhead or as big as the palm of a hand. They can construct giant fortresses or lift a thousand times their weight, fly for miles to find the right mate, or lie still for years underground.

It is estimated that there are more than one million known **species** of insects on our planet (and many more that have yet to be discovered), showing a great variety of shapes, colors, and sizes. Insects represent almost 90 percent of the living beings on the planet!

In every square mile of the earth's surface, there are 10 billion insects, a number close to the total of all the people living in the world.

Nearly 90 percent of the living beings on the planet are insects.

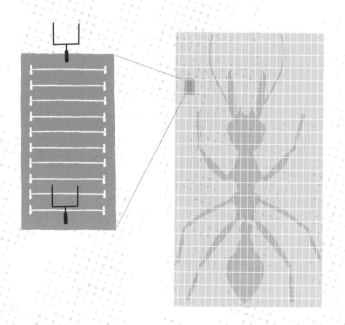

One square mile is equal to 484 football fields, and 10 billion insects can be found in that area.

The scientific study of insects and bugs is called **entomology**.

Cosmisoma

The fossils of the first dragonflies date back to the Carboniferous Period, almost 360 million years ago.

Leaf insect

5

What Is an Insect?

Insects are **invertebrate** beings, which means that they do not have a spine, and they belong to a group called **arthropods**, living things that have both an external skeleton (called an **exoskeleton**) that protects them and jointed legs.

The body of an insect has three parts: head, **thorax**, and **abdomen**. They have two **antennae** and six legs, and many of them have wings (although not all of them can fly).

Antennae _____

Compound
eyes _____

Mouthparts _____

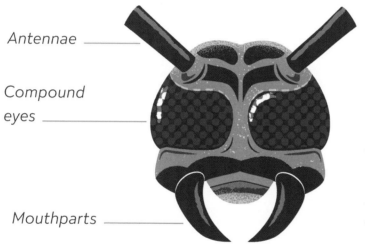

COMPOUND EYES

Most insects have big compound eyes, located on the sides of their heads. The surface of a compound eye is divided into thousands of smaller parts. Each one of them is an individual lens. The lenses take in a wide-angle view and can detect light changes and fast movements all around the insect.

WINGS

Wings are not only used for flying. They also can be used to hide, as protective shields, and as signals that call out to other insects or a warning to their enemies.

Many insects, such as butterflies and moths, have two pairs of wings: a pair of forewings (in the front) and a pair of hind wings. Beetles have a hard pair of forewings they use as protective covers and use their second pair of wings to fly. And some insects have wings but cannot fly.

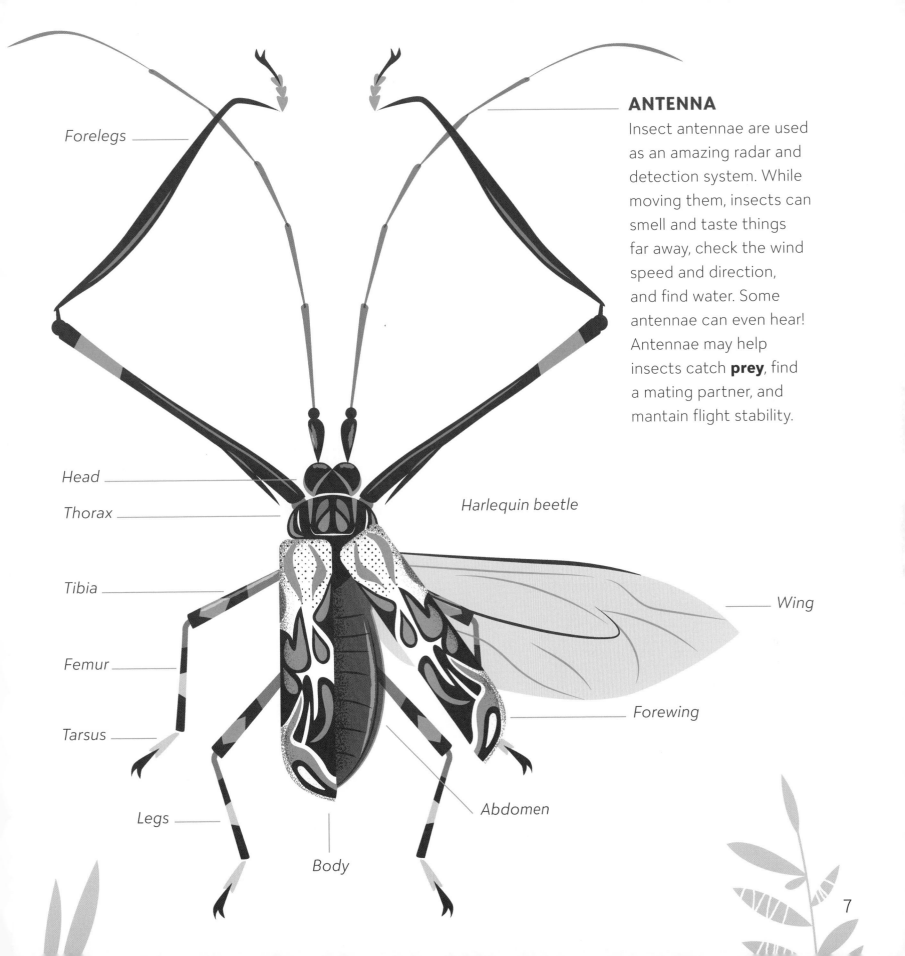

Forelegs

ANTENNA

Insect antennae are used as an amazing radar and detection system. While moving them, insects can smell and taste things far away, check the wind speed and direction, and find water. Some antennae can even hear! Antennae may help insects catch **prey**, find a mating partner, and mantain flight stability.

Head

Thorax

Harlequin beetle

Tibia

Wing

Femur

Tarsus

Forewing

Legs

Abdomen

Body

Around the World

Insects are found in (almost) every **environment** on earth, from the jungle to the desert, deep underground, and high in the mountains.

The landscapes where most insect species are found are the ones with warm, moist climates. These are rain forests and jungles.

There are fewer insects found living underwater. However, many depend on a liquid environment to nurture their young, like mosquitoes and dragonflies do. Insects like the diving beetle spend most of their time underwater, but they must return to the surface to breathe air.

The sea is the only habitat where insects are difficult to find—which is curious since it is where arthropods originated millions of years ago!

Click beetle

Treehopper

Giant swallowtail butterfly

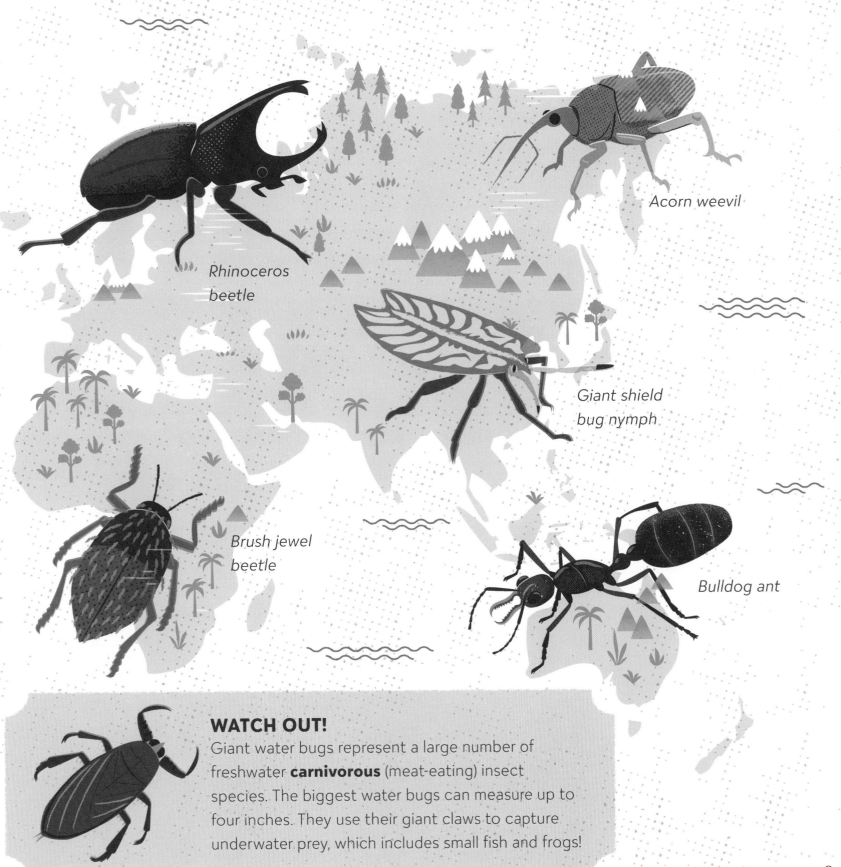

Rhinoceros
beetle

Acorn weevil

Giant shield
bug nymph

Brush jewel
beetle

Bulldog ant

WATCH OUT!
Giant water bugs represent a large number of
freshwater **carnivorous** (meat-eating) insect
species. The biggest water bugs can measure up to
four inches. They use their giant claws to capture
underwater prey, which includes small fish and frogs!

Insect Development

There are several forms of reproduction among insects, and each one is more surprising than the last. The majority of insects mate through sexual reproduction between a male and a female insect. But, like certain beetle species, some of them can be asexual, which means they don't need a partner.

Most insects are **oviparous**. That means that they lay eggs that hatch and develop into the young insect and then into the adult. This changing process is known as **metamorphosis**.

Insects that go through a simple—or incomplete—metamorphosis have three life stages. When the egg hatches, out comes a **nymph**: a baby insect that looks similar to the adult stage but smaller. The young insect may shed its skin several times up to the adult version.

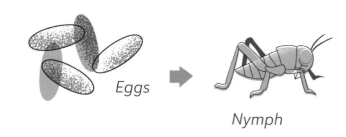

Eggs

Nymph

Adult

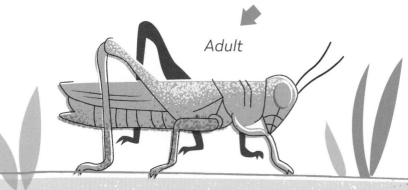

Mayfly

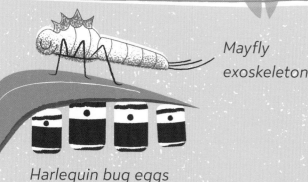

Mayfly
exoskeleton

Harlequin bug eggs

CURIOUS PARENTING
Unlike mammals, most insects tend to abandon their eggs and young to develop on their own.

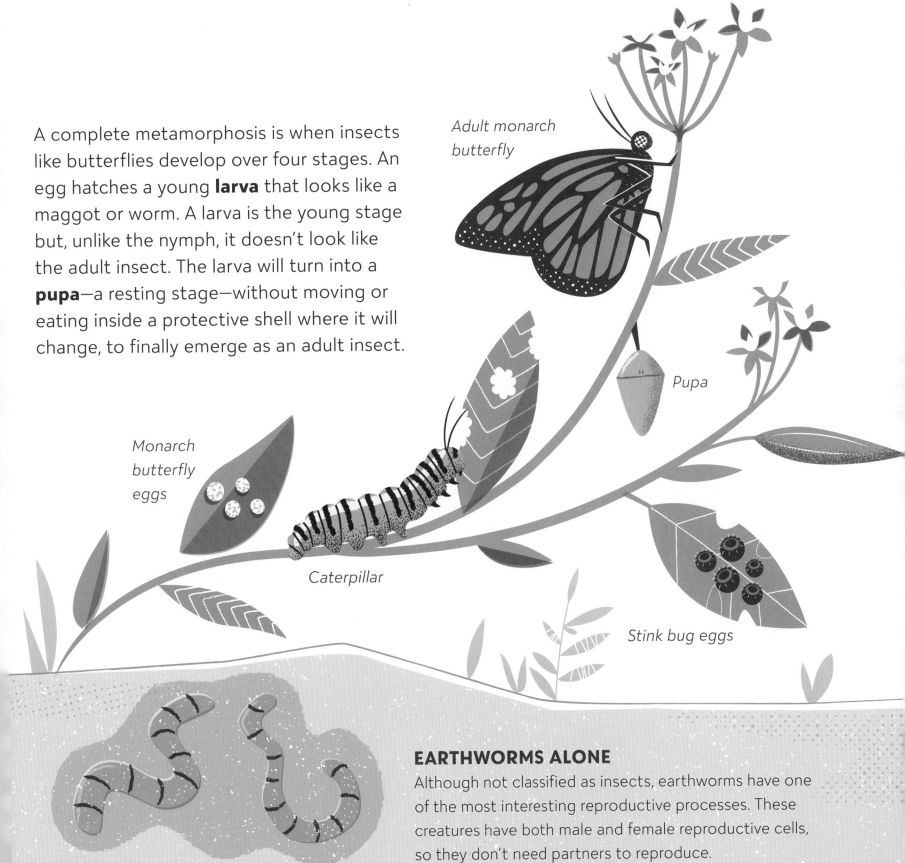

A complete metamorphosis is when insects like butterflies develop over four stages. An egg hatches a young **larva** that looks like a maggot or worm. A larva is the young stage but, unlike the nymph, it doesn't look like the adult insect. The larva will turn into a **pupa**—a resting stage—without moving or eating inside a protective shell where it will change, to finally emerge as an adult insect.

Adult monarch butterfly

Pupa

Monarch butterfly eggs

Caterpillar

Stink bug eggs

EARTHWORMS ALONE

Although not classified as insects, earthworms have one of the most interesting reproductive processes. These creatures have both male and female reproductive cells, so they don't need partners to reproduce.

Bees, the Great Pollinators

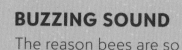

Through the process of **pollination** where they transfer tiny grains of pollen from one flower to another, some insects like bees and butterflies help grow new flowers, plants, and trees. Bees are essential all over the world!

Among the 20,000 types of bees, honeybees are the ones responsible for the honey we eat. They live in large colonies, called hives, with over 20,000 bees including the queen, the female workers who collect the pollen and feed the colony, and the male bees, called drones, whose only job is to mate with the queen.

There is only one queen in each colony, and only the queen lays eggs. If the queen bee dies, the workers can create a new queen bee by selecting a young larva and feeding it with a nutritious secretion called "royal jelly" instead of pollen or honey like the worker bees. The larva will grow into a new queen.

BUZZING SOUND
The reason bees are so noisy is because they flap their wings over 11,000 times per minute!

Honeybee

12

AFRICANIZED KILLER BEES

While their **venom** is no more dangerous than regular bees, killer bees tend to attack in larger groups, posing a greater danger to people, especially those allergic to bee stings.

CUCKOO BUMBLEBEES

These bumblebees sneak into other colonies to lay their eggs and let the workers of the established colony raise them.

Drone

THE QUEEN

The queen is the largest in the colony and has a thinner, longer body and smaller eyes than the other bees.

Each day, the queen bee can lay thousands of eggs from which new female workers and male drones will hatch.

Egg

13

Caterpillars

Caterpillars are the larval stage of the butterfly and moth insect group. These hearty eaters, most of them **herbivorous** (plant-eating), have soft bodies that can grow quickly from a quarter of an inch to five and a half inches long. During that process, some species will shed their skin up to four times—and some even eat their discarded skin!

Caterpillars have six true legs on their thoraxes and pairs of "prolegs" along the rest of their bodies. Once the metamorphosis process ends, those legs will develop into the butterfly or moth's four legs. In some species, their two rear legs will disappear after the pupa stage.

Io moth caterpillar

Saddleback caterpillar

WARNING SIGNS

Many caterpillars are **poisonous**, and their brightly colored bodies are red flags for **predators**. The saddleback caterpillar has stinging hairlike bristles on its backside. Its green and red hues function as a warning signal.

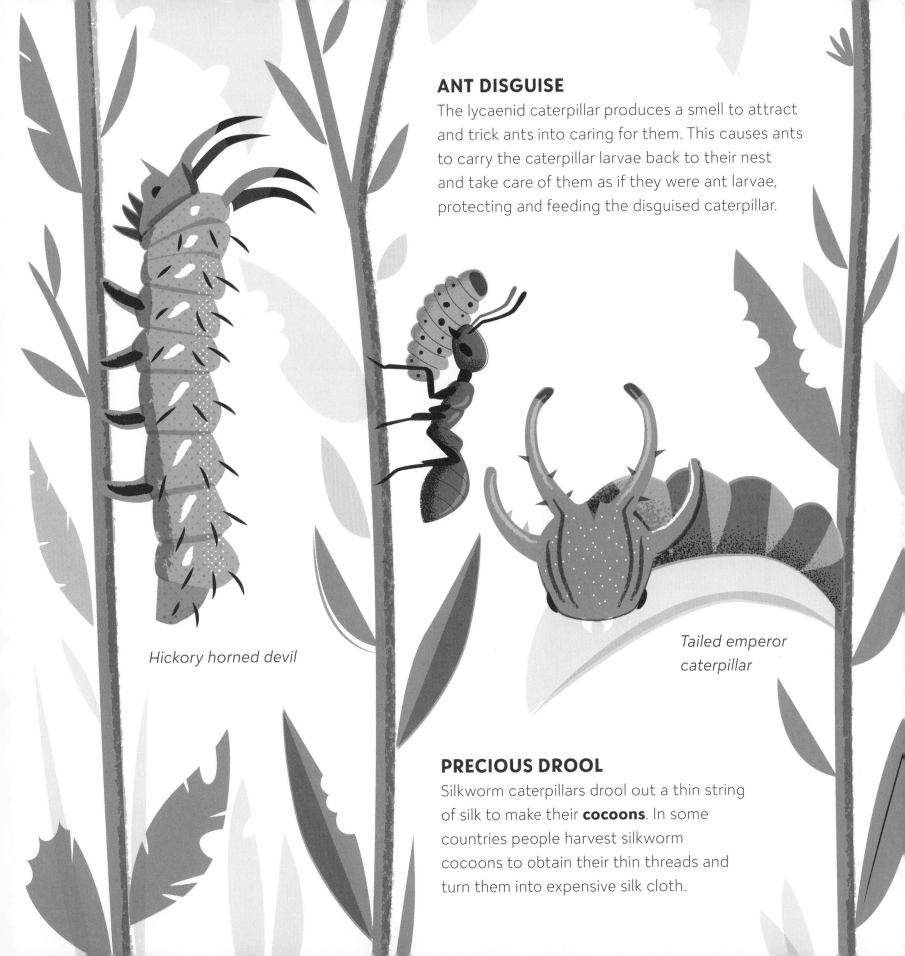

ANT DISGUISE

The lycaenid caterpillar produces a smell to attract and trick ants into caring for them. This causes ants to carry the caterpillar larvae back to their nest and take care of them as if they were ant larvae, protecting and feeding the disguised caterpillar.

Hickory horned devil

Tailed emperor caterpillar

PRECIOUS DROOL

Silkworm caterpillars drool out a thin string of silk to make their **cocoons**. In some countries people harvest silkworm cocoons to obtain their thin threads and turn them into expensive silk cloth.

Tiled Wings: Butterflies

Lepidoptera, more commonly known as moths and butterflies, are among the most popular insects thanks to the striking colors and patterns of their wings. Lepidoptera is a word that comes from ancient Greek, meaning "tile-winged."

Moths and butterflies have a complete metamorphosis, passing from the egg to the larva, then to the pupa stage, and finally to the fully developed adult stage.

Birdwing butterfly

88 butterfly

Queen Alexandra's birdwing butterfly

MIGRATION

During the fall, monarch butterflies fly more than 2,500 miles from the northeastern United States to Mexico to find warmer weather. Millions of monarchs reunite in colossal sleeping colonies grouped together on trees to stay warm during the winter.

FEEDING

Moth and butterfly mouths are shaped like tubes that unwind and help them to feed on the nectar and water found on flowers. Their mouths are adapted to collect and distribute **pollen** that plants produce.

Glasswing butterfly

Moths

Moths are usually dismissed as the more plain-looking relatives of butterflies but many moth species are actually colorful and very bright. There are many myths surrounding these creatures.

It's important to know that moths evolved long before butterflies, so they are their older ancestors. These insects have a pair of forewings and a pair of smaller hind wings just like butterflies.

Their feathery-looking antennae help moths stay oriented during flight and also help to detect possible mates. Butterfly antennae tend to be longer and thinner than moth antennae.

It is a mystery why moths are attracted to light. Scientists believe that it helps them to create a flight path, but this has not yet been proven.

And not all moths will eat your clothes! Just a small number of moth species actually eat fabric.

Leopard moth

MOTH OR BUTTERFLY?

One way to tell a butterfly from a moth is to take a look at their wings while they are resting. Moths tend to rest with their wings open, while butterflies rest with their wings closed in an upward position.

Atlas moth

Garden tiger moth

MAGIC WING POWDER

The powder moths sometimes leave behind is actually made up of tiny scales they shed from their wings over their lifetime.

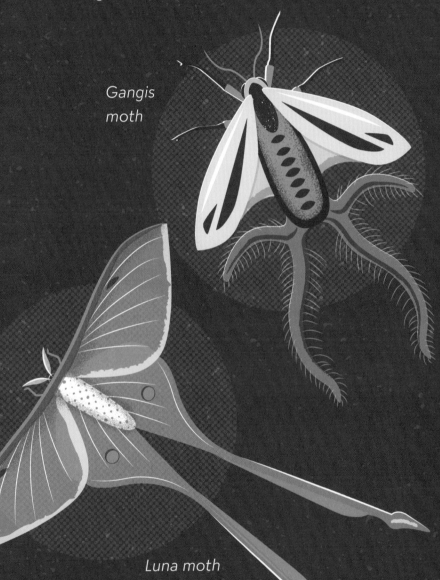

Gangis moth

THE DAY AND NIGHT MYTH

It is not true that butterflies eat during the day and moths eat at night. Some butterflies have **nocturnal** (nighttime) feeding habits. And some moths, like the hummingbird hawk moth, can be found eating during the day.

Luna moth

AVOIDING BATS

Luna moths have large twin tails on their hind wings. As the moth flies, the tails move so quickly they create a confusing sound. This affects the "radar" senses of bats, allowing the luna moth to escape any potential bat attacks.

Blue clipper butterfly

Sylphina angel butterfly

Red postman butterfly

Tiger swallowtail butterfly

Pipevine swallowtail butterfly

Parthenice tiger moth

Spanish moon moth

Long-tailed
burnet moth

Io moth

Brahmin moth

21

Scorpionfly

The scorpionfly is a strange combination of fly, butterfly, and scorpion. The distinctive tail that gives it its name is the shape of a stinger, although it does not carry poison. It is used by males to attract their mates and to scare other creatures!

The scorpionfly has a long, beak-shaped head. This is very useful in finding food among the remains of other dead insects, including those that can be found in a spider's web. Their long, jagged jaws are great for tearing up and chewing their food.

Scorpionflies are night hunters.

WE ARE EVERYWHERE!
There are around 400 scorpionfly species! They are found in areas of dense forest vegetation on every continent.

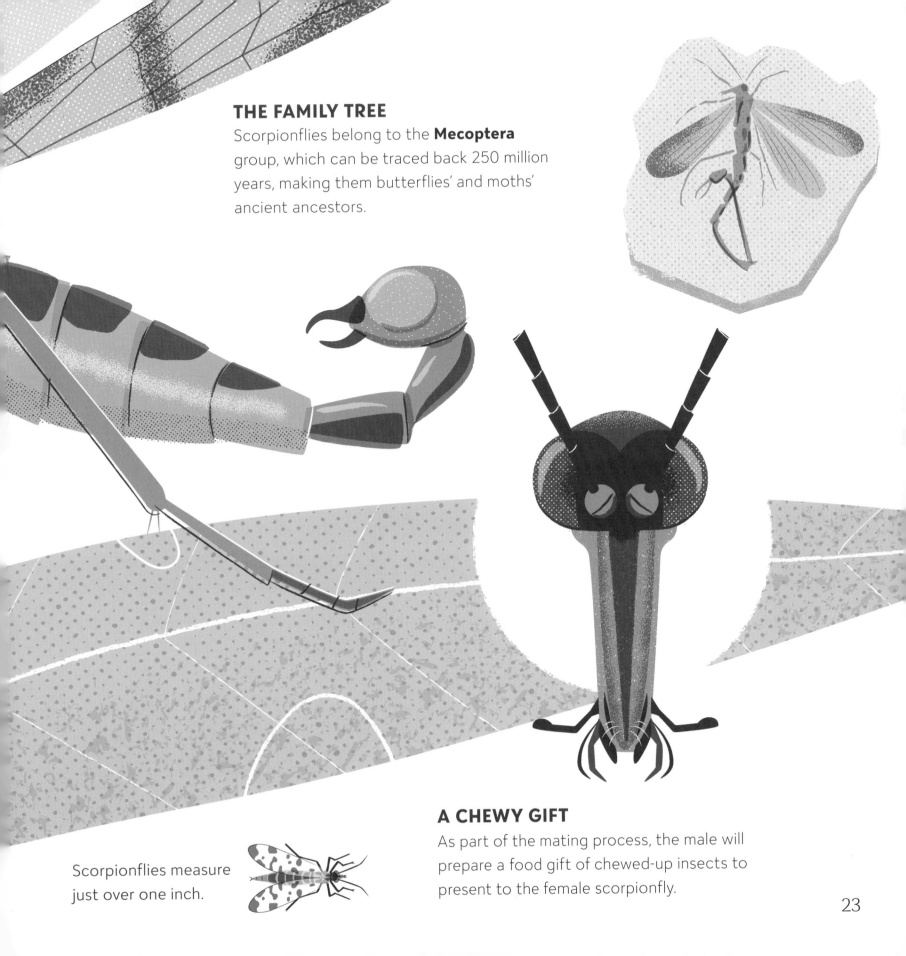

THE FAMILY TREE

Scorpionflies belong to the **Mecoptera** group, which can be traced back 250 million years, making them butterflies' and moths' ancient ancestors.

A CHEWY GIFT

As part of the mating process, the male will prepare a food gift of chewed-up insects to present to the female scorpionfly.

Scorpionflies measure just over one inch.

Among the Trees: Treehoppers

Between shrubs, leaves, and branches in the rain forest, different oddly shaped insects can be found. Treehoppers might be the most beautiful and strange among them.

Also known as "thorn bugs," these little creatures can be distinguished by the protective plate on the insect's back. These shields help the treehopper hide in plain sight, so it can be really difficult to spot them.

Their diet depends on the fluids they extract from plant stems. They drink plant juice during the day and at night. Their mouths are equipped with piercing claws, and their saliva prevents tree bark from healing, so they can continue to feed on one plant for a long time. If they find a good spot, they can stay there for a month.

Their average length is less than one inch.

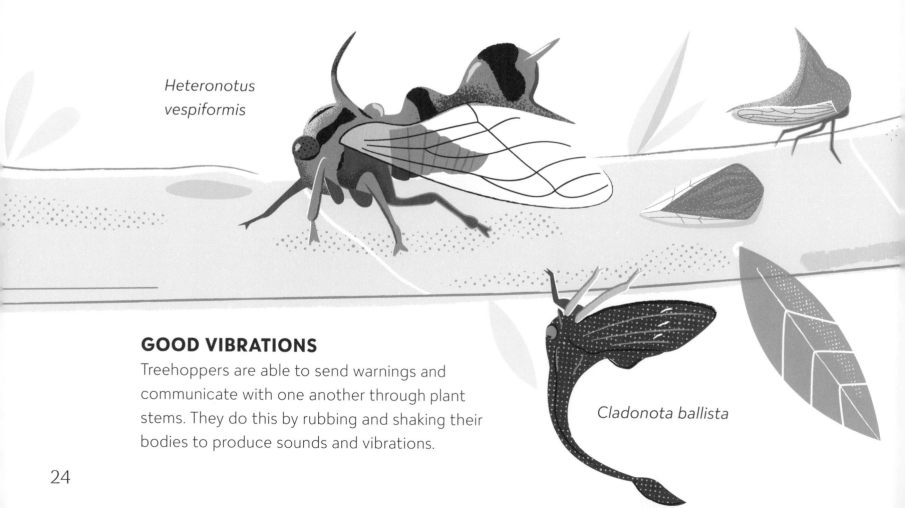

Heteronotus vespiformis

Cladonota ballista

GOOD VIBRATIONS

Treehoppers are able to send warnings and communicate with one another through plant stems. They do this by rubbing and shaking their bodies to produce sounds and vibrations.

24

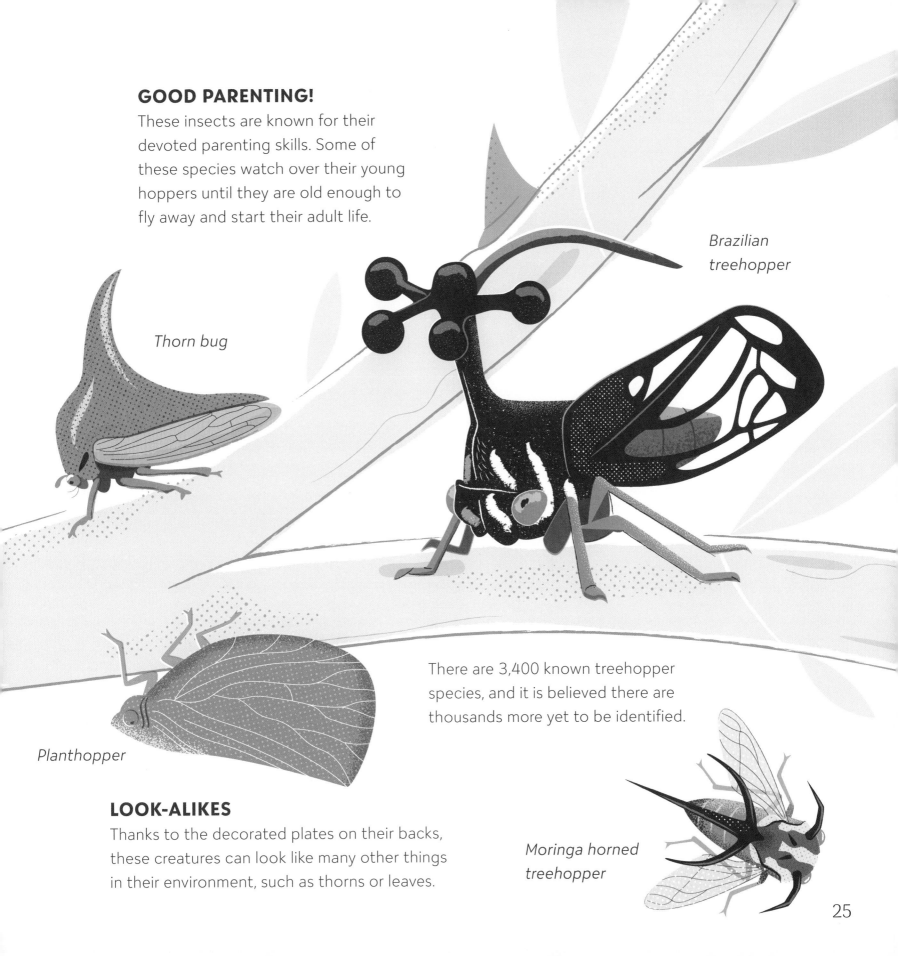

GOOD PARENTING!

These insects are known for their devoted parenting skills. Some of these species watch over their young hoppers until they are old enough to fly away and start their adult life.

Brazilian treehopper

Thorn bug

There are 3,400 known treehopper species, and it is believed there are thousands more yet to be identified.

Planthopper

LOOK-ALIKES

Thanks to the decorated plates on their backs, these creatures can look like many other things in their environment, such as thorns or leaves.

Moringa horned treehopper

Among the Trees: Beetles

Beetles belong to the largest order of insects, known as **Coleoptera**, with 400,000 species identified so far. From the sacred scarabs found in ancient Egypt to the side dishes seen on some menus today, beetles are found in every human culture.

Beetles can be identified by their strong back armor. Their forewings are stiff covers that protect the hind wings the beetle uses to fly. By spreading their fan-shaped antennae apart, they can pick up the direction of the wind currents and the odors of their food.

Beetles usually feed on plants and on live or dead animals, playing an important role in the process of soil **decomposition**. But they also represent a problem for farmers in many parts of the world since they eat every crop they find.

GIRAFFE STAG BEETLE

These giant beetles, found in Asia, Indonesia, and Java, are among the world's largest stag beetles. Half of their body length is made up of their two very long, sharp jaws that slice through caterpillars, larvae, and even other beetles. Stag beetles are powerful and aggressive and use their jaws to fight, similar to the way male reindeer use their antlers.

BEETLE-WING ART

In some ancient Asian cultures, shiny wood-boring beetle wings were used to decorate textiles, paintings, and jewelry. Since the lifespan of an adult is three to four weeks, in countries like Thailand people waited until the beetles died of natural causes to avoid killing them.

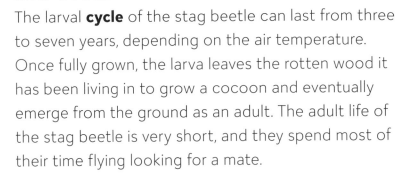

Larva

LIFE CYCLE

The larval **cycle** of the stag beetle can last from three to seven years, depending on the air temperature. Once fully grown, the larva leaves the rotten wood it has been living in to grow a cocoon and eventually emerge from the ground as an adult. The adult life of the stag beetle is very short, and they spend most of their time flying looking for a mate.

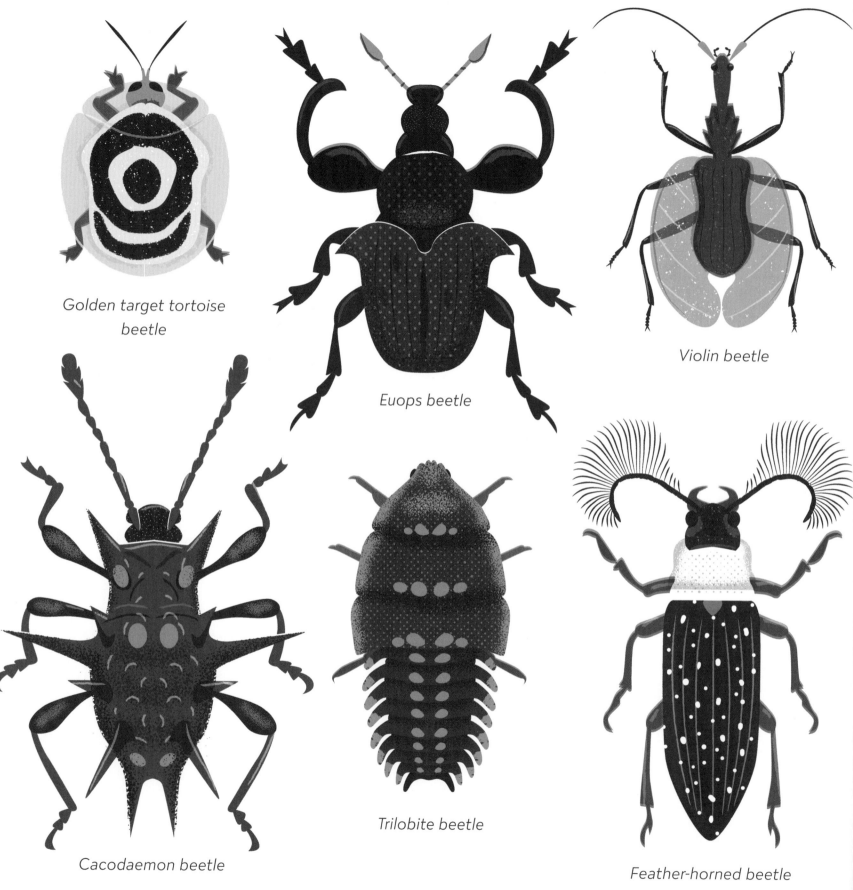

Golden target tortoise beetle

Euops beetle

Violin beetle

Cacodaemon beetle

Trilobite beetle

Feather-horned beetle

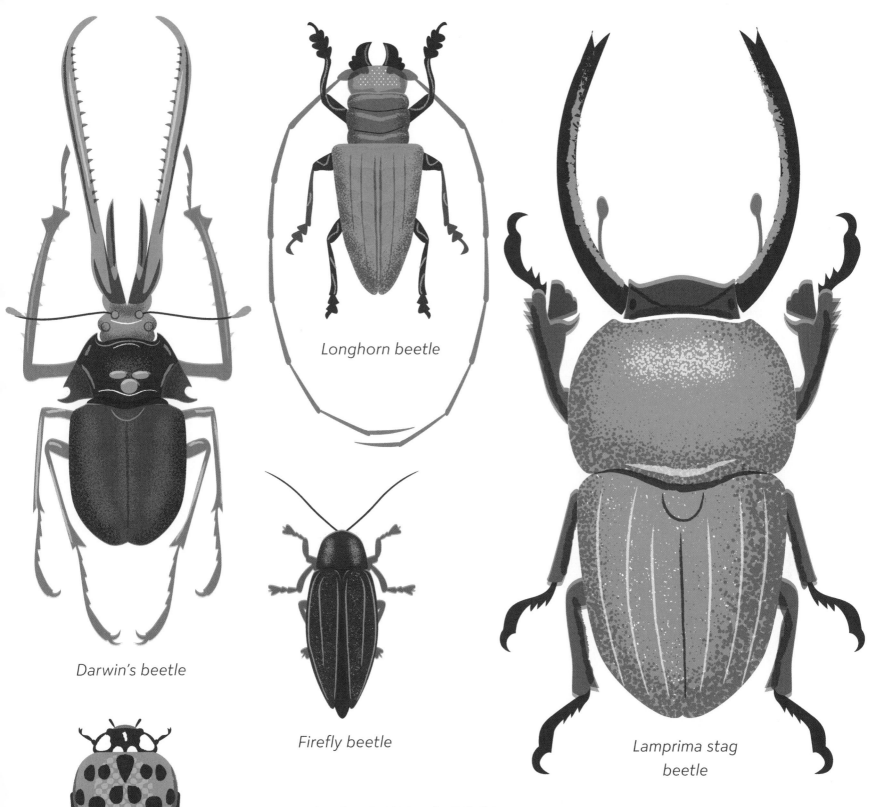

Darwin's beetle

Longhorn beetle

Firefly beetle

Lamprima stag
beetle

Ladybird beetle

FIREFLIES ARE BEETLES, TOO!

In some beetle species, the females may "flashlight" their tails to attract mates.
This is possible because of a chemical process called **bioluminescence**.

Builders Up High

Looking at insect homes can help us understand just how complex and extraordinary their lives are.

Flying insects often build their nests high up in the treetops, hanging from a branch, or even on the roof of a building. By doing this they can raise their eggs and larvae far away from a large number of predators.

But some ground insects use this same behavior, climbing trees and hanging their nests up high, to keep their eggs far away from other creatures' menus.

Weaver ants

PERFECT CIRCLE CUTS

The leaf-cutter bee takes half-moon shaped pieces of leaves and shrubs back home to create their nests.

SPIRAL HIVE

No one knows why, but the sugarbag bee in Australia makes a complex spiral-shaped beehive. A fully developed nest has 10 to 20 layers designed this way.

HANGING A NEST

Weaver ants use the sticky silk from their own larvae to "sew" the sides of a leaf together. After combining several leaves, they can create a closed nest on a tree branch instead of placing it underground like common black ants.

LOG CABIN

The bagworm moth caterpillar weaves a silk cocoon around itself before growing into its adult form. Unlike other moths, it also reinforces the outside of its cocoon using twigs, leaves, and wood to create an amazing tiny "log cabin" shelter.

PAPER WASP

This name given to several wasp species refers to the paperlike nests these insects make by chewing up wood and other plants and mixing it with their saliva to form a soft paperlike **pulp**. The pulp dries to form a sturdy nest.

Builders on the Ground

Some insects like beetles, termites, and most ants live together in large groups called colonies. Thousands of insects may live inside giant nests, whether they are built up on the ground like the termites' tall mounds or underground in infinite tunnels like the leaf-cutting ants' anthills.

ENDLESS ANTHILLS

One of the largest anthills in the world was found in Europe. It was created by the Argentine ant species and extends for more than 3,700 miles of underground tunnels and entrance mounds above the ground!

Eggs

DEADLY DECORATION

Headhunter ants decorate their nests with the heads of dead insects hanging on their walls.

Larvae

TERMITE CATHEDRAL

African Macrotermes termites build cathedral-like nests.

These structures rise up to 15 feet high, with towers that function as chimneys and outside columns that work as a kind of air-conditioning system. The queen is very comfortable here!

A termite queen can lay an egg every two seconds, day and night, for up to 10 years!

JUNK BUG

The lacewing larva, which will become a net-winged insect, carries all its belongings on its back. But what looks like garbage is actually this cold-blooded killer's victims' dead bodies used as **camouflage**!

33

Fire Ants

The name "fire ant" couldn't be more accurate: These ants have red bodies and a really painful bite, which feels similar to being burned by fire.

Originally from tropical areas in South America, the fire ant was accidentally introduced into other continents around 1930 by boat along with a cargo shipment. This is why they are also known as Red Imported Fire Ants (RIFA).

They are considered to be among the most invasive and aggressive species in the world because they don't have many predators.

Giant colony swarms can be quite dangerous. In cases of highly allergic people, the poisonous bite of the red ant can be deadly.

THE HEAD HUNTER

The phorid fly lays its egg inside a fire ant's back. Its larva will hatch and move toward the head of the ant to feed. About three weeks later, the fly larva is finished with its meal. The now-empty head of the fire ant falls off, and a little phorid fly will appear.

COMPLETE METAMORPHOSIS

Fire ants begin as eggs, which become larvae when hatched. Then they change to a pupa stage and finally grow into adult ants.

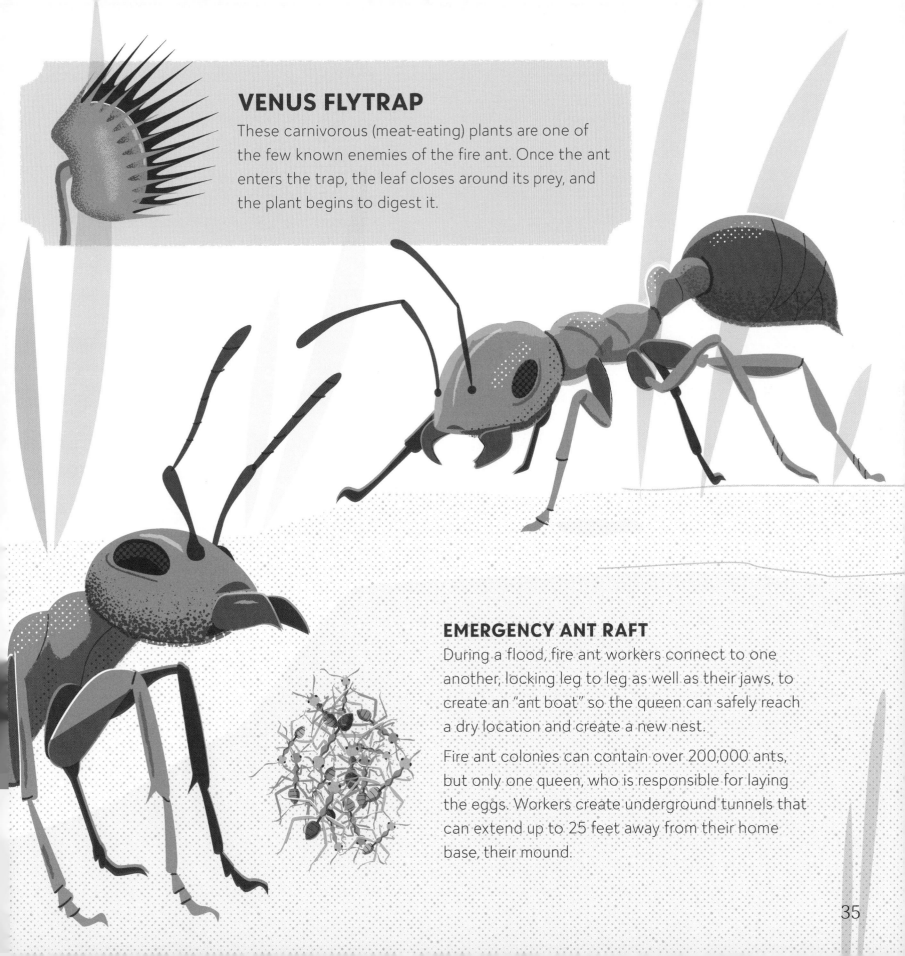

VENUS FLYTRAP

These carnivorous (meat-eating) plants are one of the few known enemies of the fire ant. Once the ant enters the trap, the leaf closes around its prey, and the plant begins to digest it.

EMERGENCY ANT RAFT

During a flood, fire ant workers connect to one another, locking leg to leg as well as their jaws, to create an "ant boat" so the queen can safely reach a dry location and create a new nest.

Fire ant colonies can contain over 200,000 ants, but only one queen, who is responsible for laying the eggs. Workers create underground tunnels that can extend up to 25 feet away from their home base, their mound.

Defense Systems

Green huntsman spider

There are many ways to hide, escape, or deflect a predator attack. (Beetles, for example, have evolved their wings into protective shields.) Some insects use bright colors, loud sounds, or threatening postures to defend themselves. Some have poisonous defense systems, others leave a foul taste or smell, and still others make use of sharp spines or aggressive tactics.

These warning signals are beneficial for both predator and prey, since both avoid being harmed.

BUG SAVE THE QUEEN!

When a predator gets near their queen, weaver ants protect her by piling up on top of her. They cover the queen completely, creating a defensive ant mountain around her.

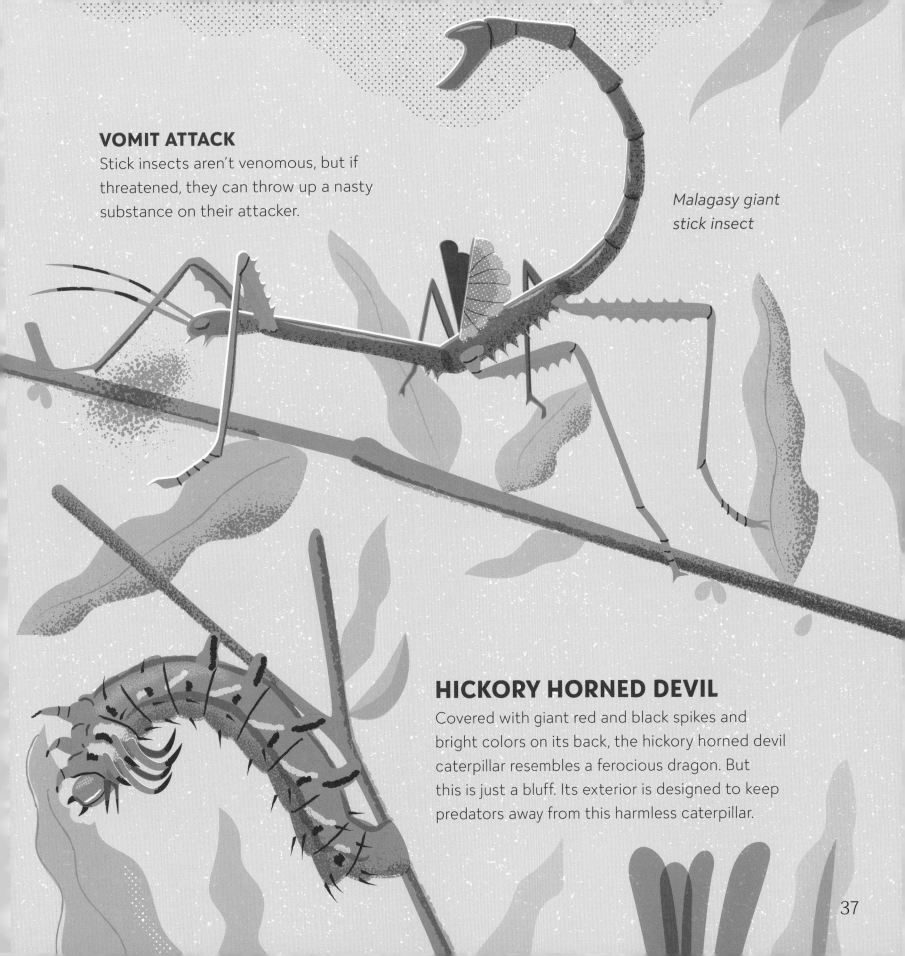

VOMIT ATTACK

Stick insects aren't venomous, but if threatened, they can throw up a nasty substance on their attacker.

Malagasy giant stick insect

HICKORY HORNED DEVIL

Covered with giant red and black spikes and bright colors on its back, the hickory horned devil caterpillar resembles a ferocious dragon. But this is just a bluff. Its exterior is designed to keep predators away from this harmless caterpillar.

Now You See Me, Now You Don't

Some species of insects have the ability to hide in plain sight. This is called camouflage.

They are able to blend in with the environment and vegetation that surrounds them, becoming almost invisible, either to protect themselves from other predators or to stalk their prey and hunt.

Insects have evolved so that their external appearance might look similar to the environment where they live, to the point that some of these creatures are almost impossible to spot.

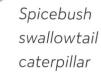

Spicebush swallowtail caterpillar

WATCH OUT FOR THE SNAKE!

The green and brown spicebush swallowtail caterpillar can inflate its body parts and enlarge its black spots to look like big "eyes." In this way, it imitates a snake perfectly.

SPINY LEAF INSECT

The spiny leaf insect belongs to a well-camouflaged group of insects called phasmids, the stick insect group. They look like dead leaves to easily blend in with their surroundings.

DISGUSTING VEST!

Bird dropping treehoppers larvae look like bird poo . . . who dares to take a bite?

Praying Mantis

This alien-faced insect is usually found in warm regions, along tropical zones in every continent.

Mantises are carnivorous (meat-eating) and are great predators: They can turn their heads around to look behind them for prey. Lurking between leaves to ambush their victims, they strike rapidly using long front legs that are equipped with small spikes.

A large mantis can eat prey as big as mice, lizards, and even very small birds like hummingbirds! Moths, crickets, grasshoppers, flies, and other insects are also on the menu.

Some mantis species can stand up to five inches tall. They usually shed their skin several times over a lifetime.

ONE EAR

The mantis is the only living being with only one ear . . . and it is in their thorax! They depend on their amazing sight and ability to detect vibrations in order to catch prey and protect themselves from predators, including frogs.

It is believed that praying mantis kung fu was developed based on the striking and jabbing motions of this insect!

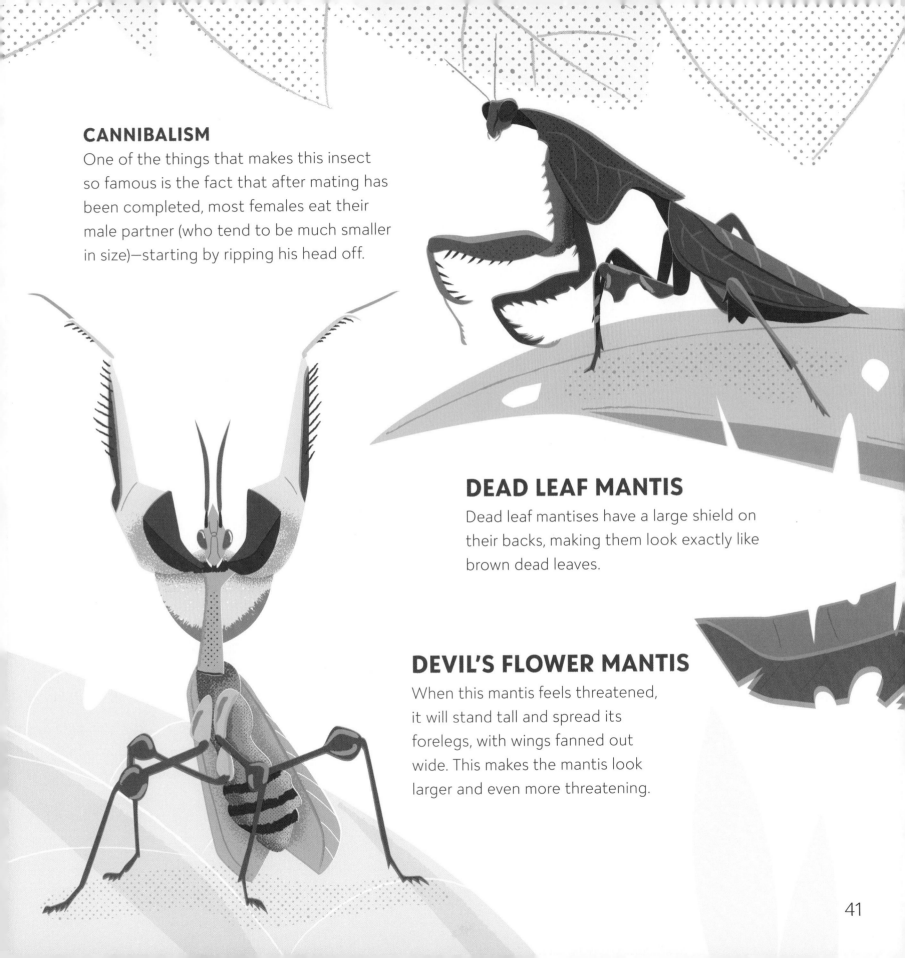

CANNIBALISM

One of the things that makes this insect so famous is the fact that after mating has been completed, most females eat their male partner (who tend to be much smaller in size)—starting by ripping his head off.

DEAD LEAF MANTIS

Dead leaf mantises have a large shield on their backs, making them look exactly like brown dead leaves.

DEVIL'S FLOWER MANTIS

When this mantis feels threatened, it will stand tall and spread its forelegs, with wings fanned out wide. This makes the mantis look larger and even more threatening.

Spiders Are Not Insects!

Over 45,000 spider species have been identified around the world. Spiders are among the most feared creatures on the planet, even though most of them pose little or no danger at all to human beings. In fact, some are helpful in controlling pests on crops and farms. But spiders are not insects! They are **arachnids**.

Unlike insects, arachnids have eight legs and do not have wings or antennae. Spider bodies are divided into only two parts, instead of three parts like insects.

Ticks, scorpions, and spiders are part of this group of arthropods that feed by sucking the juices of their victims. They usually feed on other animals and insects.

Spiders can have stingers or claws, and can even deposit venom on their prey.

Whip scorpion

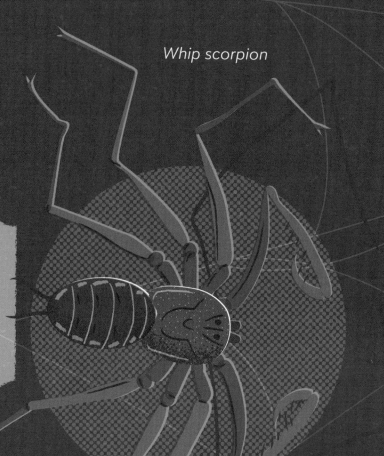

SPIDER SILK

Spiders produce different types of silk from their abdomen, the largest part of their bodies. The silk can be used to create a safe line (or drag line) to move from place to place. Another type of silk is sticky enough to catch prey or to wrap around a captured meal.

PEST CONTROL

One way to naturally control insect pests in crops is to introduce spiders (most insects' natural predator). This has been done successfully in apple farms and rice fields.

Peacock spider

Camel spider

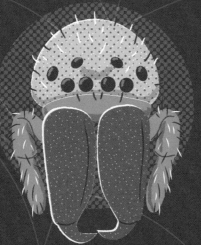

POOR VISION

Although they have up to four pairs of eyes, spiders do not have great vision. They mostly detect their prey by sensing sound vibrations.

43

Bugs vs. Insects

People use the words *bug* and *insect* interchangeably, but this is not entirely accurate.

All bugs are insects but not all insects are true bugs.

Like insects, true bugs have three-part bodies, six legs, two antennae, and compound eyes. The key difference is in their mouths: Unlike insects, bugs have no teeth and drink the juices of a plant or of their prey through a mouth shaped like a straw.

Bugs also have a pair of stiffened front wings.

LADY NO-BUGS
Ladybugs are not bugs! They are insects from the beetle family.

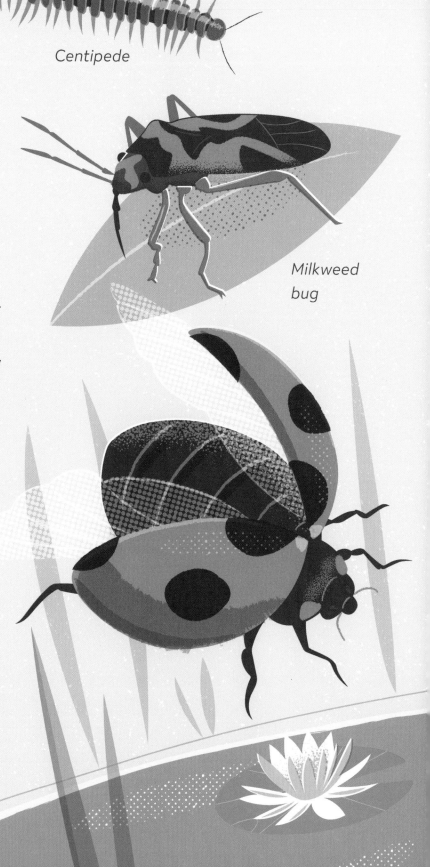

Centipede

Milkweed bug

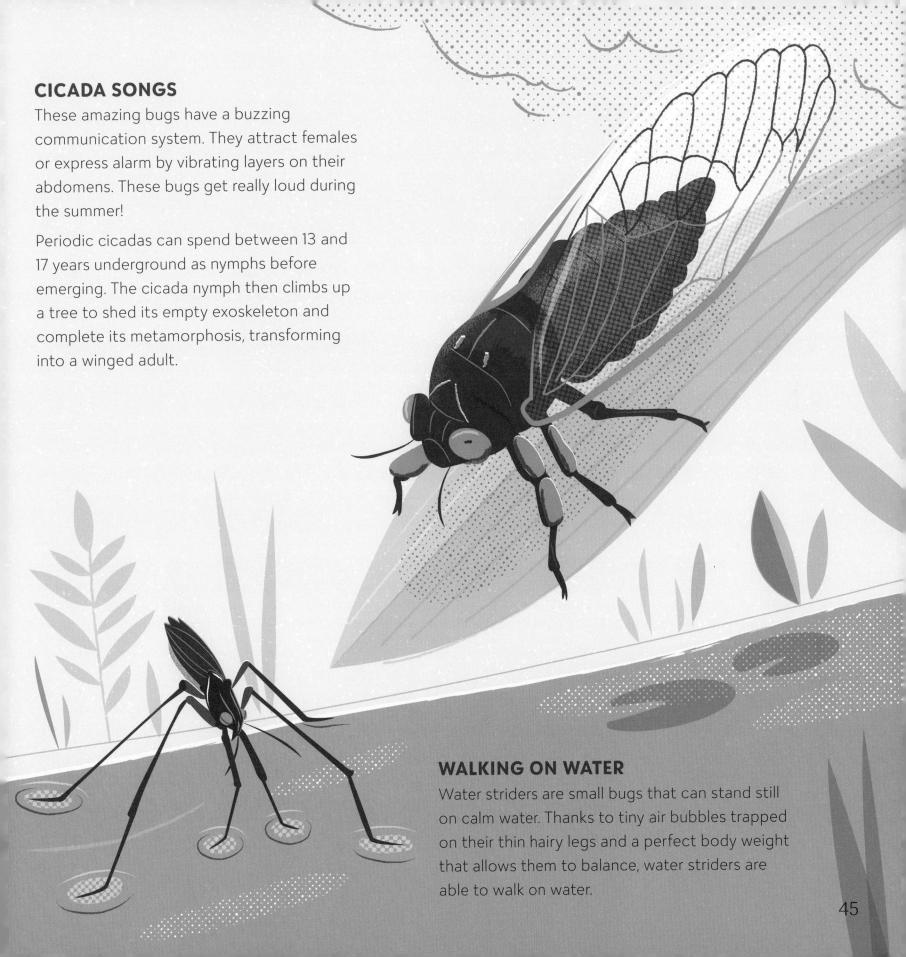

CICADA SONGS

These amazing bugs have a buzzing communication system. They attract females or express alarm by vibrating layers on their abdomens. These bugs get really loud during the summer!

Periodic cicadas can spend between 13 and 17 years underground as nymphs before emerging. The cicada nymph then climbs up a tree to shed its empty exoskeleton and complete its metamorphosis, transforming into a winged adult.

WALKING ON WATER

Water striders are small bugs that can stand still on calm water. Thanks to tiny air bubbles trapped on their thin hairy legs and a perfect body weight that allows them to balance, water striders are able to walk on water.

Danger: Poison!

There are several insects and arachnids that are dangerous to humans due to their poisonous bites. While some are harmful, others can be deadly.

Black widow spider

Wheel bug

ASSASSIN

The wheel bug uses its needlelike beak to stab its prey and inject it with a paralyzing venom. It uses its straw-like mouthpart to drain the dead insect's body fluids for its dinner.

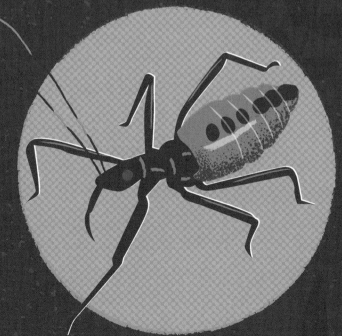

BLISTERING BUGS

Blister beetles secrete a painful poison that they use as a defensive agent. This substance can cause blistering on the skin of its enemies. Eating it can cause convulsions or even death. Warning! Don't try to handle or catch any blister beetles.

WORLD'S DEADLIEST SPIDER

The funnel-web spider (originally from Australia) is the most dangerous spider to human beings. Its powerful venom can cause death within 15 minutes.

Orb-Weaver Spiders

If you find a wheel-shaped web in your garden, you may see a beautiful orb-weaver spider close to the edges. These spiral webs can measure up to 24 inches across, even though the orb-weaver spider is very tiny. They average less than a third of an inch for females. The males are even smaller!

These little spiders can be recognized by the variety of bright colors and detailed patterns they wear on their backs.

Orb-weaver spiders can be found in Southeast Asia and India, but they also have been introduced by accident into the southern United States. These ferocious looking spiders are harmless to humans but a real problem to their predators.

The long-horned orb-weaver is also known as the curved spiny spider.

Spiny orb-weaver

SPINY ORB-WEAVER

These orb-weaver colors and spiked shaped body act as warning signal. If a predator catches it with its mouth, the spines on its back will stick in the predator's mouth. While trapped, the orb-weaver will leave a horrible-tasting liquid until the predator spits the spider out and retreats.

Their long body horns are still a mystery— experts are not sure what their purpose is.

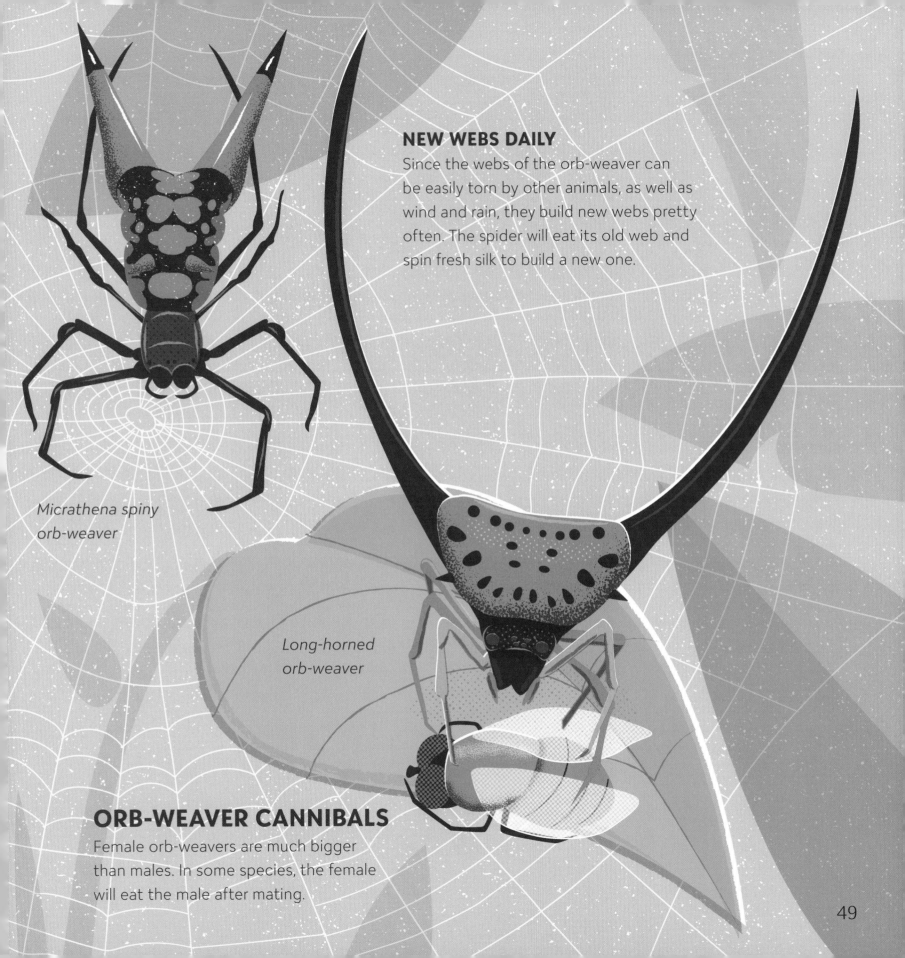

*Micrathena spiny
orb-weaver*

NEW WEBS DAILY

Since the webs of the orb-weaver can be easily torn by other animals, as well as wind and rain, they build new webs pretty often. The spider will eat its old web and spin fresh silk to build a new one.

*Long-horned
orb-weaver*

ORB-WEAVER CANNIBALS

Female orb-weavers are much bigger than males. In some species, the female will eat the male after mating.

49

Giant vs. Tiny

The insect world is very diverse. Some insects can be larger than an adult's hand. And you might need a magnifying glass to find others.

Which are the largest insects?
Which are the smallest?

THE STRONGEST CREATURE ON EARTH

The Hercules beetle lives up to its name. Not only is it the largest of its kind, but it can also lift up to 850 times its weight!

GOLIATH SPIDER

The Goliath spider is so big that it is known as the "birdeater" because of its large size and big appetite. It can eat a hummingbird, but it usually feeds on smaller animals, like frogs and lizards.

GIANT STICK INSECT

The phasmid, better known as the stick insect, may measure over 20 inches long (bigger than this book when open!), making it the longest insect in the world.

SCARLET DWARF

This tiny red dragonfly's body measures only 0.78 inches. It can be found in Asia.

PIGMY BLUE

The wingspan of these butterflies is less than half an inch, making it the world's smallest butterfly.

FAIRYFLIES

These wingless male "fairy wasps" are the smallest insects in the world, with an average length of only five one-hundredths of an inch!

LEAFHOPPER NYMPH

These nymphs are so small (around half an inch) that the best way to find one is by looking for their strange tails. They are actually formed from a waxy substance the nymph secretes to put on a flashy show and avoid being eaten.

Plagues and Swarms

A plague is a disease that can be widespread by animals, insects, or bugs and affects other living beings' health, and in some cases causes death. Our world depends on insects to pollinate plants, to fertilize the soil, to help eat dead animals, and as food for other species in the food chain. But human life can be affected in many ways by insects and bugs, too.

An insect swarm is a large group of insects moving and feeding together, able to destroy entire crops and gardens in just a few days.

MOSQUITOES

Mosquitoes are among the most dangerous insects to humans. They spread diseases, including yellow fever, dengue, and malaria, by carrying the viruses in their saliva and infecting people they bite while draining their blood.

TEN-STRIPED SPEARMAN

The ten-striped spearman, or colorado potato beetle, is a major pest of potato crops in North America. The female is very fertile, able to lay up to 500 eggs in a four-week period, a real problem for potato farmers.

LOCUST CLOUDS

Locusts are short-horned grasshoppers that are usually solitary creatures. But in some cases, when environmental conditions are just right, these insects change their behavior. They can even change color and body size, and begin moving in groups, forming a swarm of millions, ravaging crops and devouring all the plant life they encounter.

They are especially attracted to the cereal grain crops found across the continent of Africa, but locust clouds also form in North and South America.

CHAGAS-SPREADING BUGS

Some assassin bugs, like bedbugs, are responsible for spreading the Chagas disease in rural areas of Mexico, Central America, and South America. Chagas disease can be deadly for young children.

Conservation

Insects participate in all the processes that are related to life on our planet. They consume and break down all kinds of living matter. They are necessary to pollinate and spread plant life accross the entire planet. They contribute in bringing air to the soil while digging their homes and to fertilizing the ground while carrying their food.

So, without insects, it would be difficult to maintain life!

Even if we see them every day, today there are currently fewer insects than at any other time since humans have been on earth. And change is needed if we want life to continue on our planet, not just for bugs, but for all life forms.

Leaf mimic katydid

Ithomiini butterfly

ECOSYSTEM HELPERS

An ecosystem is composed of living beings like animals and plants, as well as nonliving things like water, soil, and rocks. Together these form a community of life in a single area or region. In a particular ecosystem, insects provide many solutions: They pollinate plants, spread plant seeds, maintain the soil, fertilize while feeding, help decompose dead creatures, and provide a food source to other animals.

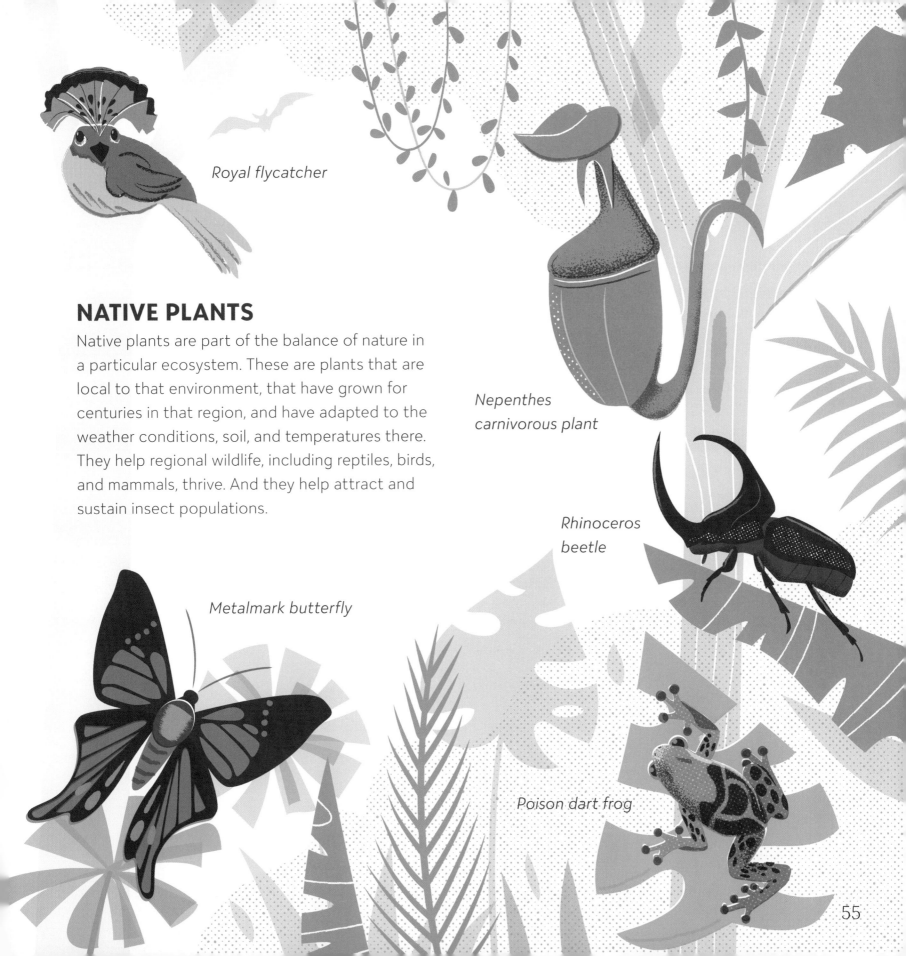

Royal flycatcher

NATIVE PLANTS

Native plants are part of the balance of nature in a particular ecosystem. These are plants that are local to that environment, that have grown for centuries in that region, and have adapted to the weather conditions, soil, and temperatures there. They help regional wildlife, including reptiles, birds, and mammals, thrive. And they help attract and sustain insect populations.

Nepenthes carnivorous plant

Rhinoceros beetle

Metalmark butterfly

Poison dart frog

Glossary

Abdomen: The body part located behind the thorax. Inside it are the organs used to breathe, the organs that digest food, the system in charge of pushing out waste, and the reproductive system.

Antennae: The pair of sensory organs that are sensitive to touch, smell, and even sounds in some insect species.

Arachnid: The group of eight-legged arthropods like spiders and scorpions. Unlike insects, arachnids have bodies that are divided in two sections and don't have antennae or wings.

Arthropod: The group of invertebrate animals that have jointed feet and bodies that are divided into segments, covered by an exoskeleton which is used as shield or shell.

Bioluminescence: The ability of some living things to produce light. It is a chemical reaction where the energy that is produced is released as a light. Some species use this light to attract their prey or find mating partners.

Camouflage: An adaptation—usually of color or patterns—that helps certain animals "disappear" into the environment in which they live.

Carnivore (carnivorous): An animal or plant that eats animals.

Cocoon: A covering case or shell made by young insects to protect them while growing from a pupa into an adult.

Coleoptera: The group of insects with hardened front wings, consisting of beetles and weevils. The word comes from the ancient Greek meaning sheath.

Cycle: The series of changes that repeats itself in the same order is known as a cycle. It is a series of stages a living being goes through in their life while developing, and it is the same series of changes for every generation. All animals have a similar life cycle: They are born, grow from young to adult, some will have newborns, and in the end they will die.

Decomposition: The breakdown of living beings like plants, animals, or insects after they die. Decomposition is the process where the dead body is reduced into simpler, tiny pieces with the passage of time, and those pieces become part of the soil.

Entomology: The science of insects. The people who study insects and their world are called entomologists.

Environment: Everything that surrounds us forms the environment. All animals and plants, weather conditions, soil, rocks, and water are parts of the environment.

Exoskeleton: The hard cover or shell that supports and protects an animal's body.

Herbivore (herbivorous): An animal that only eats plants and their juices. They also feed on fruits, roots, or seeds.

Invertebrate: The groups of animals without an internal skeleton or backbone.

Larva: The insect juvenile stage, right after it hatches from the egg and before it changes into its adult form.

Mecoptera: A word that comes from the ancient Greek, meaning long wings.

Metamorphosis: The transformation or change that some animals and insects go through during their life, from the immature young form to the adult form in two or more different stages.

Nocturnal: Animals that are awake and active at night and that rest during the day. They hunt, feed, or mate at night and sleep and hide during the day.

Nymph: The young stage of some insects and other invertebrates. For insects that go through an incomplete metamorphosis, the larval or juvenile insect stage is also called a nymph. The nymph looks like its adult form but much smaller.

Oviparous: Animals that reproduce by laying eggs, from which the young will develop and hatch outside their parents' bodies.

Poison (poisonous): A substance that causes harm or even death when it is eaten, smelled, touched, or injected.

Pollen: A fine powder produced by some male plants that can be released into the air or carried by some insects and animals to other plants to form seeds, and new plants can grow from those seeds.

Pollinate (pollination): When the pollen from the male part of a plant reaches the egg of the female part of a plant to form a seed, the pollination process is completed.

Predator: An animal that hunts, catches, and eats other live animals to eat. The top predator is the one that is not prey for other animals.

Prey: Animals that are hunted for food. The prey is what the predator eats.

Pulp: A soft, wet mass of material.

Pupa: The middle stage of an insect's development, while changing into the adult. A pupa is protected inside a cocoon without eating or moving, going through lots of internal changes and external like growing out wings. The pupa stage only occurs in insects that go through a complete metamorphosis.

Species: A specific kind of organism. Species is a basic classification for living things that all share common characteristics. All animals or plants that are the same kind are one species: Dogs are one species. Wolves are another species. Humans are another species.

Thorax: The part of the insect body between the head and the abdomen. The thorax is the anchor point for legs and wings. In human and animal bodies, the thorax is the chest.

Venom (venomous): A kind of poison used by animals. It is made inside the body of the venomous animal and injected by sting or bite as a toxic fluid into another animal's body.